ULTIMATE
Smoky
Mountains

ULTIMATE
Smoky
Mountains

DISCOVERING THE GREAT NATIONAL PARK

Andrew Kyle Saucier

Photography by Tony Sweet

Globe
Pequot

Guilford, Connecticut

Globe
Pequot

An imprint of The Rowman & Littlefield Publishing Group, Inc.
4501 Forbes Blvd., Ste. 200
Lanham, MD 20706
www.rowman.com

Distributed by NATIONAL BOOK NETWORK

British Library Cataloguing in Publication Information available

Library of Congress Cataloging-in-Publication Data available

ISBN 978-1-4930-2931-0 (hardcover)
ISBN 978-1-4930-2932-7 (e-book)

∞™ The paper used in this publication meets the minimum requirements of American National Standard for Information Sciences–Permanence of Paper for Printed Library Materials, ANSI/NISO Z39.48-1992.

Printed in the United States of America

There are trees here that stood before our fore-
fathers ever came to this continent; there are
brooks that still run as clear as on the day the
first pioneer cupped his hand and drank from
them. In this Park, we shall conserve these trees,
the pine, the red-bud, the dogwood, the azalea,
the rhododendron, the trout and the thrush for
the happiness of the American people.

–President Franklin D. Roosevelt, September 1940 at the
Dedication of Great Smoky Mountains National Park

TABLE OF CONTENTS

INTRODUCTION

I believe this is the most beautiful place on Earth–
this portion of the Southern Appalachians along
the Tennessee–North Carolina line that we call
the Great Smoky Mountains–I am not alone. It is
a landscape as deeply shrouded in mythology as
it is in the mist, or "smoke," from which it gets its
name. Today the National Park Service maintains
solid roads and trails that crisscross the landscape,
but much of the park remains wild and remote, not
only in its deepest recesses and most distant mountains, but in the imaginations of the thousands of
tourists who visit each year.

Over a century ago, when Horace Kephart first
traveled to the Smokies, scholarly knowledge on
the region was little advanced. In *Our Southern
Highlanders*, a seminal work on the people of
the region, Kephart remarked, "When I prepared,
in 1904, for my first sojourn in the Great Smoky
Mountains, which form the master chain of the
Appalachia system, I could find in no library a guide
to that region."

Kephart spent some eighteen years learning
that life for the people who lived in the Smoky
Mountains during the early 1900s was scarcely
more modern than it had been during the early
1800s. He found more commonalities to the people
of Davy Crockett's time than of his own, a modern,
industrial age led by indomitable characters such
as Theodore Roosevelt, Henry Ford, and John D.
Rockefeller.

Change was imminent, however. Kephart was not alone in recognizing what could be gained from preserving these mountains for future generations. He began to document the people and the landscape that had, for so long, remained unchanged.

The great forest wherein it nestled is falling . . . before the loggers' steel. A railroad has pierced the wilderness. A graded highway crosses the county. There are mill towns where newcomers dwell. An aeroplane *[sic]* has passed over the county seat. Mountain boys are listening, through instruments of their own construction, to concerts played a thousand miles away. . . . Old ways, old notions, old convictions perhaps, must give place to new ones. . . . They die hard, those old ways, in the mountains. Some of them were good ways, too.

Ever since the Great Smoky Mountains National Park was officially established on June 15, 1934, the scholarly works and guides to the region–the ones Kephart "could find in no library"–have abounded. Kephart would have easily found them in any library had he not died in 1931. And while no book on a place so spectacular and immense could ever truly be comprehensive, we've sought to capture, through words and images, some of the Great Smoky Mountains' most endearing natural features, animals, and stories.

Yet, in the end, no book ever written can or will catalogue what may be the park's most profound legacy–the power to bring out the wild imagination in each of us, the ruggedness that lies deep within the forests of our hearts and the mountains within our souls.

Newfound Gap Road

If you only had a single afternoon to spend in Great Smoky Mountains National Park, you're likely to have taken one of two drives: the Cades Cove Loop or Newfound Gap Road. Newfound Gap Road, US-441, runs between Gatlinburg, Tennessee, and Cherokee, North Carolina, bisecting the deep heart of the Great Smoky Mountains and transporting motorists up, over, and back down the very spine of Appalachia itself.

Newfound Gap Road is constructed to allow visitors to travel with the landscape, not straight through it. It traverses some of the most spectacular scenery viewable from the comfort of a car. All along the wayside, pull-offs offer travelers a chance to stand at vistas of incredible elevation. The panoramic Appalachian landscape of serrated ridges and recessed valleys pale from blue to gray until they literally vanish beyond what the eye can see. The road culminates at Newfound Gap itself, right on the Tennessee–North Carolina line. Here, at this relatively low gap in the mountains for which the road is named, visitors stand at an elevation of approximately 5,046 feet above sea level.

The road was completed around 1932, and at the Newfound Gap parking lot stands the Rockefeller Memorial, where Franklin D. Roosevelt dedicated the park in September of 1940. During his speech, Roosevelt said, "It is good and right that we should conserve these mountain heights of the old frontier for the benefit of the American people."

All these decades later, we recognize that it was not only for the benefit of the American people that these mountain heights were conserved, but for the benefit of the entire world.

Clingmans Dome

A spur of Newfound Gap Road is the skyway to Clingmans Dome. At roughly 6,643 feet above sea level, travelers enter into an entirely different climate than in the valleys down below. Clingmans Dome is the highest point in the national park, as well as in the state of Tennessee. At the very pinnacle stands the famed concrete observation tower, constructed to replace the wooden tower built here by the Civilian Conservation Corps.

On a rainy day, you may very well find yourself shrouded by the very clouds themselves. On a clear day, the immensity of the 360-degree view begs description. The visible world seems to disappear over the horizon, as if you could actually see the curvature of the Earth.

THE OBSERVATION TOWER AT CLINGMANS
DOME CARRIES VISITORS UP OVER THE
TREETOPS AND OUT TOWARD THE STARS.
Sean Pavone/iStock

Cades Cove

They came from old pioneer stock. Generations who, by toil and sweat, worked the sun down into the western sky, taming this isolated wilderness. Tree by tree, their forebears cleared the woodlands in the valley to raise crops and graze livestock. They were removed from the rest of the world except for the rugged mountain roads that had in previous generations been warpaths and hunting trails of the Cherokee. By and by they created a thriving community in Cades Cove. They had simple home-steads in which to raise their families, and churches in which to worship. There were roads that led to Maryville and into Western North Carolina.

The year that Tennessee became a state, present-day Cades Cove was still part of the Cherokee Nation, and it remained so until some date between 1818 and 1821. But it was not long until the European-turned-American settlers came, and their descendants continu-ously inhabited the Cove for nearly 115 years between settlement and the cre-ation of the park. Then the federal and state governments began buying land tracts from the residents of the Cove. As the families moved away one by one, they left behind the structures that had made up their communities, and to this day, the National Park Service maintains the ones that did not fall and has recon-structed many of the ones that did.

Undoubtedly the most popular park activity, the Cades Cove Loop scenic drive meanders through the community that once thrived here–past a working gristmill, barns of various styles, log homesteads, and churches of several Christian denominations. These structures tell the stories of the people who are now long gone.

The Wildflowers

The Great Smoky Mountains wild-flower displays are renowned world-wide. Each spring, a wave of blooms sweeps over the park. Typically, they peak around mid-April, but as with the fall foliage, this cannot be taken as gospel. Several factors affect the timing each year. Yet you can count on one hard-and-fast rule to help pinpoint this event: While several species bloom all summer, many of the wildflowers' most vibrant colors begin to fade as the trees fill in with leaves.

It is said that there are more kinds of flowering plants in the Great Smoky Mountains than in any other national park, and while the Smokies are particularly well known for their incredible mountain laurel, flame azalea, and rhododendron, the National Park Service estimates that the total number of flowering plant species exceeds 1,600.

The Wildflowers   25

These wildflowers have names as wild and varied as their shapes and colors, such as spring beauty and bloodroot; smooth and false Solomon's seal; bishop's cap; several kinds of trillium, including Catesby's and Vasey's; Robin's plantain and the dwarf crested iris; Dutchman's breeches and squirrel corn; bleeding heart and blue phlox; jack-in-the-pulpit and the squawroot.

One of the first flowers to bloom in the park comes as early as late February or early March: trailing arbutus, with tiny pink-white flowers. Horace Kephart, ever the keen observer, wrote, "In summer the upper mountains are one vast flower garden: the white and pink of rhododendron, the blaze of azalea, conspicuous above all else, in settings of every imaginable shade of green."

Black Bears

There are literally hundreds of unique species of animals protected by the national park. Of them, the most popular is undoubtedly the black bear, who has become the de facto mascot of the Great Smoky Mountains National Park.

It is estimated that there are roughly 1,500 bears in the park. While the average male bear can weigh as much as 250 pounds, bears over 600 pounds have been found here. They are adept climbers and can be seen lounging in the boughs of trees in a fashion most people would associate with apes, though they cannot swing from limb to limb. Summer is feasting season, and because these bears are omnivores, they can be spotted eating a wide array of foods, from acorns and berries to salamanders from the streams.

It is imperative to remember that viewing wildlife in the park comes with considerable responsibility. Although the bears typically appear docile and calm, they are, of course, wild animals. There is never an excuse for approaching a bear. Not only is it dangerous—it is illegal.

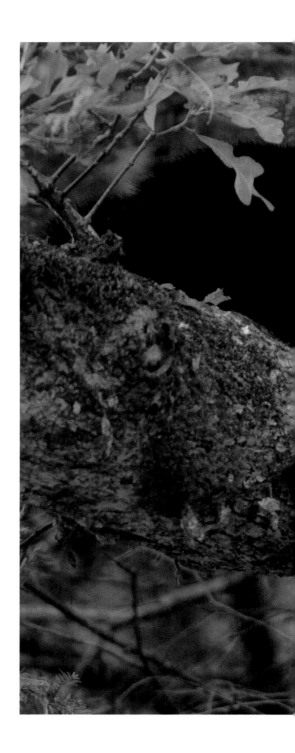

Elk

There was never any question of why the eastern elk disappeared from the Southern Appalachian Mountains. The now oft-told story of overhunting and habitat encroachment pushed them to extinction. By the time the national park was founded and these lands were protected, it was simply too late.

But beginning in 2001, the National Park Service began relocating Manitoban elk in the Smoky Mountains as part of a park-wide effort to reestablish these beasts into a landscape in which they once flourished. Twenty-five animals were released into the national park. The next year, twenty-seven more joined the herd. As of today, the reintroduction has been a complete success, and with each mating season, the elk multiply and spread throughout the mountains.

These elk, especially the herds of Cataloochee Cove, have become very popular. Herds are also commonly seen in the meadows around Oconaluftee, near Cherokee, North Carolina. And while the black bear remains the Great Smoky Mountains' mascot, the elk have, in their relatively short tenure as park residents, made a home in the hearts of all who come to see them.

Fishing

The Great Smoky Mountains are big enough to mean a lot of different things to a lot of different people. For some people, it's all about trout.

Of the roughly 2,900 miles of streams in the park, a little less than a quarter of them are sizable enough for the park's native fish species to flourish. But as it turns out, that's plenty. These mountain streams remain one of the last natural wild trout habitats in the entire eastern United States.

The effort to foster and maintain this healthy ecosystem is as old as the Civilian Conservation Corps, which, in the early years of the park, labored tirelessly to restock these once overfished streams. Thanks to the parks department, this effort never stopped.

Today, anglers cast or wade into the swift, cool waters in hopes of hooking a big one. Some days they reel in a foot-long brown trout. Some days end without so much as a nibble. Either way, it's hard to imagine a more pristine environment in which to throw out a line.

Autumn

It begins on the mountain-tops. At 6,000 feet and higher, the climate is more like that of Vermont, 1,000 miles to the northeast, than it is to Gatlinburg in the valley below.

Around mid-September, the trees—cherry, birch, beech, and more—at higher elevations may begin to change, while the mountain slopes and valleys below remain lush and green. Soon, early- to mid-October, as the temperatures and humidity levels begin to drop in earnest, change creeps down the faces of the mountains.

As October begins to wind down and early November settles in, the valleys and the hollows and the trees overhanging the swift mountain rivers—hickories, red and sugar maples, and sweetgums—reveal vibrant displays of color. While high above, where it all began a month or more ago, the summits begin to appear bare and ready for winter.

Joe Kramer/Flickr

Elkmont Ghost Town

The tracks of the Little River Railroad had been laid to bring in loggers and haul out timber, but Colonel Townsend, enterprising owner of the Little River Lumber Company, recognized the potential of recreational tourism. As talks of a national park began in earnest, fewer logs filled the freights for export and, increasingly, tourists were imported.

Long before the park was established, the Appalachian Club at Elkmont was frequented by the wealthier travelers aboard the Little River Railroad. It was a private vacation community in the mountains, a sort of exclusive outdoorsmen's club with road names like Millionaire's Row and Society Hill. Many of the club's members were, of course, prosperous and influential. It is said that one such member, after being inspired by a trip to Yellowstone, began to rally for the establishment of a national park in the Smokies. His fellow club members joined him in his efforts.

Over the decades since the park was founded, the buildings on this once private, now public land began to disappear back into the mountainous landscape. Elkmont became a deserted town in the woods. Buildings in various stages of dilapidation started to slouch into the weeds. A cemetery stood in a far clearing while the roads turned to mud tracks. It began to assume the look of a place far more sinister than its origins would suggest, and over the years it became known to the park's visitors as the Elkmont Ghost Town.

The town seemed destined to disappear altogether, until 1994, when many of the buildings were put on the National Register of Historic Places. This, of course, changed the National Park Service's duties on the subject

of what was now known as Elkmont Historic District. Today, they have restored the Appalachian Clubhouse and even some of the private cottages. The Appalachian Club is, at least nominally, again open for business.

Kevin Adams Photography

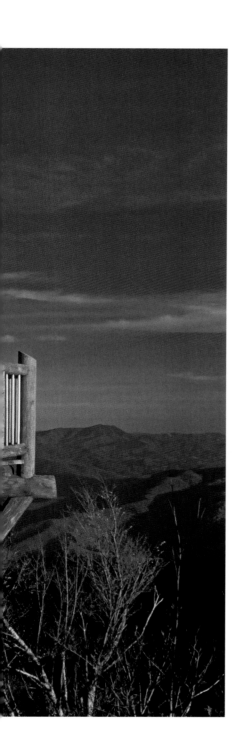

Mount Cammerer Fire Tower

Arno Berthold Cammerer dedicated his professional career to the National Park Service, serving as its third national director during the critical early years when the lands of the Great Smoky Mountains National Park were being acquired and developed. In return, the park dedicated an entire mountain to him.

Squatting at the top of Mount Cammerer stands a defunct fire tower. Built in the 1930s by the Civilian Conservation Corps, the structure is not a true fire tower, but rather a lookout hut. Yet, as can be common with names, the misnomer stuck.

Today, it is no longer used for its original purpose. However, those who will endure the roughly eleven-mile round-trip hike to the summit and back will have no trouble recognizing that the structure was well placed. Hikers are rewarded with a 360-degree panoramic view of the mountains of the Tennessee–North Carolina border, the same view afforded to park rangers and fire lookouts of decades past.

At one time, there may have been as many as ten such fire towers or lookouts in the Great Smoky Mountains National Park. Only four stand today, Mount Cammerer included. The other three—Shuckstack, Mount Sterling, and Cove Mountain—are proper, honest-to-goodness fire towers.

WHETHER YOU HIKE, BIKE, OR DRIVE, TRAVELING TO THE
TOP OF THE TRAILHEAD OR CLIMBING A LOOKOUT TOWER
IS WELL WORTH THE EFFORT FOR AN UNOBSTRUCTED
VIEW OF THE PARK'S KALEIDOSCOPIC COLORS.
Sean Pavone/iStock

Sunrise & Sunset

In years past, even before the park was founded, watching the sun rise at Myrtle Point on Mount LeConte was a kind of initiation for visitors to the Smoky Mountains. Photographs were taken and distributed nationwide, even worldwide, depicting the scene. And while a sunrise as seen from Myrtle Point is undoubtedly a scene of incredible beauty, it is not the park's sole vantage. In truth, every mountaintop in the park is an amazing place from which to watch a sunset or sunrise—from Clingmans Dome to Mount Guyot or any other.

It is also a spectacle to witness the course of the sun from where the earliest Cherokee and frontier settlers would have most often seen it, from the valleys and bottomlands. At sunset, the shadows of trees grow long in the golden hour and the mountains themselves grow deeper in hue until they begin to blacken and disappear altogether against the darkening sky. Soon, you can only see them by lying flat on the ground and sky-lighting them against the stars.

The Forests

Theodore Roosevelt was among a long line of admirers of the forests of the Great Smoky Mountains, believing them to be "the heaviest and most beautiful hard-wood forests on the continent." The pristine woodlands that existed across this region when the Cherokee first arrived here were immense. They remained so as the first European-turned-American settlers moved into the region in the generations before industrialization. Without exaggeration, the entirety of what is today encompassed by the national park's boundary was completely forested, with small exceptions, such as the Bald Mountains and Alum Cave Bluffs.

Horace Kephart wrote that: "When [botanist] Asa Gray visited the North Carolina mountains he identified, in a thirty-mile trip, a greater variety of indigenous trees than could be observed in crossing Europe from England to Turkey, or in a trip from Boston to the Rocky Mountain plateau."

It was a woodland bounty that would eventually be the inspiration for its own destruction. Logging interests moved into the region with great enthusiasm. They cleared huge swaths of old-growth timber and hauled the logs out on newly built railroads. With the creation of the national park, the logging industry eventually vanished for good, but not before approximately two billion board feet of lumber had been harvested.

Thanks to the founding of the Great Smoky Mountains National Park these forests remain a national treasure, and the incredible diversity of species that entranced Asa Gray, Horace Kephart, Theodore Roosevelt, and millions of others can thrive once again.

The Balds

There is a great mystery to the balds, these rounded mountaintops that seem inexplicably bereft of the trees that cap nearly all the other summits. Are they somehow natural meadows? Were some of them cleared by man for mountaintop grazing or use as hunting camps? Were there giant prehistoric bison or mastodon that fed upon the vegetation, leaving nothing but grass? No satisfactory answer has appeared to finally quell the speculation. Yet their allure is undeniable.

There are several such balds in the Great Smoky Mountains, with many more existing across Southern Appalachia, outside the bounds of the park. Some of the balds that existed at the time of the park's creation have slowly become forested again. Others have not. As for Andrews and Gregory Balds—which may be the park's two most well-known and often visited—the National Park Service deliberately maintains their baldness, such that some joke that they're actually shaved.

Because these balds are at least partially if not completely clear of trees, their summits provide sweeping views of the surrounding landscape uncommon to other summits of similar altitude. This fact was not lost on author and artist Robert Mason, who was speaking of the view from Gregory Bald when he said: "No artist could paint it. To do so he would need to compete with the Master Painter using the heavens for a canvas, the sunset and rainbow for the palette, purple mists and winds out of the west for brushes."

Kevin Adams Photography

The Foothills Parkway
& Look Rock

Welcome to Tennessee's oldest unfinished infrastructure project. The two wings of the Foothills Parkway—the southwestern section connecting the tiny hamlet of Walland with the Chilhowee Lake impoundment by traversing Chilhowee Mountain and the shorter northeastern section stretching across Green Mountain in Cocke County to link the town of Cosby with Interstate 40—do not meet in the middle. At least not yet.

ehrlif/iStock

When and if the two wings of the Foothills Parkway are connected, the drive will be an incredible seventy-odd miles through the relatively low, but beautiful foothills that run the entire length of the Great Smoky Mountains National Park. While the project is stalled and today remains indefinitely incomplete, any traveler upon either wing will tell you that although the two wings may not connect, a drive on either is no less spectacular for it. Perhaps the most popular and oft-traveled of the two wings is the slightly longer southwestern section, in no small part thanks to Look Rock, an immense observation tower at the very pinnacle of Chilhowee Mountain.

Sean Board/iStock

Chimney Tops

The natural features of the Great Smoky Mountains–the streams and summits, gaps and coves–have borne many names. Some of these names, such as Chimney Tops, are more obviously inspired than others. Lore tells us that as European and American frontiersmen first laid eyes on these rocky mountaintop spires, they were reminded of chimneys and named them so. And that before them, the Cherokee called them *Duniskwa'lgun'yi*, which is thought to translate to "Gap of the Forked Antler." Today the name Chimney Tops–or sometimes simply, the Chimneys–has stuck, if for no other reason than it is easier to pronounce than the name given by the Cherokee.

Years ago, trail-goers used to be able to scrabble up steep grades over loose rock, all the way to the pinnacle of the mountain for an unimpeded view. Unfortunately, the Chimney Tops Trail and the surrounding area were badly damaged by a wildfire in 2016. The blaze destroyed 17,000 acres of national park land and parts of nearby Gatlinburg, Tennessee. It also killed 14 people and forced thousands to evacuate.

Though the pinnacles were too damaged to allow climbers access, the National Park Service has worked hard to design and develop a new section of the trail that includes a viewpoint from which to observe the Chimney Tops, and a gathering area for hikers. The new Chimney Tops Trail was reopened with much celebration in the Fall of 2017, ensuring that visitors can continue to enjoy one of the park's most popular hikes for generations to come.

Alum Cave Bluffs

Horace Kephart recalled that, "Seldom does one see even a naked ledge of rock. The very cliffs are sheathed within trees and shrubs, so that one treading their edges has no fear of falling into an abyss." But like the balds, the Alum Cave Bluffs are the exception. Here Kephart would not only see a naked ledge of rock, but he could literally stand beneath it.

Alum Cave is, without a doubt, one of the most recognizable hiking destinations in the park. However, as with many other natural features here, its name is actually a misnomer. It is not a proper cave, but rather a bluff, a hollowed-out space beneath an overhanging ledge. The hike to the top is made particularly interesting by Arch Rock, a formation holed by a tunnel and stairs that lead up and around. There is also the possibility of viewing fairly rare birds that are known to live here, including peregrine falcons, which may be the only such falcons in the entire park.

In the past, before these lands fell under federal protection, mineral deposits along the Alum Cave walls were highly sought after at various points and by various interests. During the American Civil War, the Confederate government used this location for the mining of ingredients necessary to make gunpowder.

Photos credit Kellyvandellen/iStock

Alum Cave Bluffs   59

Two Roads

Throughout the park, you will see many tracks. Deer or even elk hooves leave their distinct shapes. The paw imprint of a bear cannot be confused with any other animal. You will even see the tracks of humans, who typically leave the waffle-print of hiking boots. But rarely will you see any tracks left by tires.

As early as the 1920s, before these lands were federally protected, visitors and residents alike began to notice tire tracks left behind on the muddy, rutted routes that were traditionally nothing more than wagon paths. Today, most of the interior of the park is off-limits to motor vehicles, so those few places that do permit them are prized among off-road enthusiasts and otherwise adventurous motorists.

Rich Mountain Road is such a place. Considered "primitive and unimproved" by the National Park Service, which, in essence, means unpaved and prone to being blocked by uncleared obstacles, it is a one-way road leaving Cades Cove and winding a full twelve miles to Townsend. To be sure, this is no blacktop highway. But Rich Mountain Road is generally considered a comparatively easier road to navigate than its rougher cousin, Parsons Branch Road.

Unlike Rich Mountain Road, Parsons Branch is nominally paved with gravel, rutted and often muddy, susceptible to washouts, potholes, and uncleared obstacles. It runs something like eight miles between Cades Cove and US-129 along a bottomland route carved by Parsons Branch.

The road runs along its namesake stream, which can easily flood out of its banks. This makes it considerably more hazardous than Rich Mountain Road–and much more appealing to those seeking an off-road thrill. The road continuously fords the stream, so motorists can quite easily become stranded and mired in mud. During storms, trees are known to fall across the right-of-way. That being said, a typical drive on Parsons Branch Road is not actually dangerous. Those fueled by a considerable amount of enthusiasm, and aided by a four-wheel-drive vehicle, can and do negotiate it with little or no real issue.

Two Roads   61

Roaring Fork Motor Nature Trail

Like Parsons Branch Road, the Roaring Fork Motor Nature Trail is named for the mountain stream that dictates its course. The name hints at the stream's tendency to be one of the fastest-flowing wild streams in the entire park, especially following the frequent heavy rains of summer.

The Motor Nature Trail cuts a rough course along a five-and-a-half-mile loop through immense hardwood forests, past some of the park's most popular and unique waterfalls, and by backwoods historic structures.

At the trail's entrance, along Cherokee Orchard Road, you will find the Noah "Bud" Ogle Nature Trail. This mountain homestead hiking tour is almost completely enclosed by hardwood forests. Unique to "Bud" Ogle's homestead is one of the last surviving tub mills of the Smokies, a mill house and grindstone system once common to these mountains but long since vanished.

The Motor Nature Trail itself can easily become a full day's excursion, at the discretion of the traveler. Just past Ogle's farm is the Rainbow Falls Trailhead, which is undoubtedly one of the park's most popular hiking trails and waterfalls. Yet the most unique—or, at the very least, most uniquely named—waterfall within the park is Place of a Thousand Drips, which lies along the route.

(Top) groveb/iStock

The Waterfalls

Thousands of feet up the wooded slopes, from rainfall or springs sourced deep in the belly of the mountains themselves, mere rivulets search out the path of least resistance. As they surge downward, bound for the bottomlands, they combine to form creeks or branches of rivers. And then it happens. They come to a rock ledge or a cliff with nowhere to go but over.

Because of the steep gradient and heavy average rainfall common throughout the park, the Great Smoky Mountains are replete with waterfalls. Credit for the tallest waterfall in the park generally goes to Ramsey Cascades, although some seasoned hikers dispute its height. In total, the water falls for about 100 feet before pooling at the bottom. Among the park's most significant waterfalls are many that plummet eighty feet or more, although not always in a single, contiguous section, including Rainbow Falls, Juney Whank Falls, Laurel Falls, Hen Wallow Falls, and Mingo Falls.

But the park's tallest waterfalls may not be the most unique. On the Roaring Fork Motor Nature Trail is the aforementioned Place of a Thousand Drips. A relatively small amount of water cascades down an intricate course of rocks, creating an incomprehensible pattern over its twenty- to thirty-foot drop. Hence the name. There is no telling just how many tiny falls there are. Depending on the rain, a more appropriate name might be Place of *Ten* Thousand Drips.

ONCE HOME TO THE LITTLE RIVER LUMBER COMPANY
IN THE EARLY 1900S, TREMONT AND MIDDLE PRONG
FALLS (PICTURED ABOVE) NOW HOST CAMPERS
AND DAY HIKERS AT ONE OF THE MOST BEAUTIFUL
BACKCOUNTRY CAMPSITES IN THE PARK.

The Mountain Farm Museum & Mingus Mill

The National Park Service has helped preserve some of the history and culture of the people who resided in the Great Smoky Mountains before the creation of the park, specifically the lives of the European-turned-American settlers. Two of the finest examples, outside of Cades Cove, are the Mountain Farm Museum and nearby Mingus Mill.

The structures of the Mountain Farm Museum were collected from throughout the park and reconstructed near Cherokee, North Carolina, in the 1950s. Among them are a log farmhouse, corncribs, a smokehouse, and other structures imperative for survival at an isolated mountain homestead. Nearby is the historic Mingus Mill, built on that very location in 1886. Unique from other gristmills in the area, Mingus Mill used a waterpowered, cast-iron turbine in lieu of the more common waterwheel to propel its machinery and grind grain. Together, the Mountain Farm Museum and Mingus Mill provide immersive experiences into the lives of the Smoky Mountain settlers.

Oconaluftee & the Museum of the Cherokee Indian

Inside the Oconaluftee Visitor Center, visitors can view museum exhibits on the Cherokee, the European and American settlers, and, most recently, the Civilian Conservation Corps who lived and worked in the park during the Great Depression.

The visitor center was purposefully constructed just a few miles from the town of Cherokee, North Carolina, and the Qualla Boundary Reservation, home of the Eastern Band of Cherokee Indians. The Cherokee are an undeniable and immensely important part of the history of these mountains. While it is difficult to pinpoint exact numbers, estimates of the total number of Cherokee in and around the Southern Appalachian Mountains before settlement range from 25,000 to much higher. Their villages and towns were located along rivers in the valleys, and they hunted and foraged in the mountains.

Courtesy of the Museum of the Cherokee Indian

CHEROKEE FRIENDS MIKE CROWE JR., JARRETT WILDCATT, RICHARD SAUNOOKE, AND SONNY LEDFORD (LEFT TO RIGHT) DISCUSS ELK SIGHTINGS WHILE DRESSED FOR A NATIVE EVENT AT THE CHEROKEE HOMESTEAD.

Through trade, war, and treaties, their localized culture became increasingly exposed to that of the Europeans and then the Americans. Over time, their society came to increasingly resemble that of their white neighbors as they formed a written language, founded a government system modeled after that of the new United States, adopted subsistence agriculture as well as chattel slavery, and converted to Christianity in considerable numbers. None of this was, in the end, enough to satisfy the clamor among the Americans for their removal, culminating in the tragic exodus of many native people along the Trail of Tears. In spite of this, many stayed—and some returned. Today their descendants inhabit the Qualla Boundary, and the town of Cherokee.

Cooling Off

Visitors flocked to the Smoky Mountains to escape the searing summer heat long before the national park was created. The opportunity to spend time in the cooler mountain climate is one reason the Appalachian Club in the Elkmont Historic District was such a popular summertime destination for wealthy Knoxvillians. The average temperature during the summer months in Knoxville–only about forty miles away–can easily hover between 85°F and 90°F, with an equal percentage humidity. July and August can be brutal, with air so thick it feels as if you are actually swimming. People escaped to the Smokies the same as we do today, flocking to the mountain peaks on a scenic drive or hike, where the temperatures and overall climate are similar to that of New England.

In an effort to stay cool, visitors may want to take their cue from the salamander. The Great Smoky Mountains have been called the Salamander Capital of the World. Scientists suppose that as many as thirty or so species of salamander exist in the park, an impressive number for a single ecosystem. They inhabit the 2,100 miles or so of streams that stay cool, even in the height of summer, or they live in the deepest cove forests where, under the canopy's umbrella, the forest floor is shaded all day long.

Fontana Dam

Impounding the Little Tennessee River to create Fontana Lake in North Carolina, the Fontana Dam is the largest concrete hydroelectric dam in the eastern United States. Constructed during the tumultuous 1940s, it provided electricity to the Tennessee Valley's vital wartime industries. Not without some irony, the dam is named for the town it destroyed, which now lies at the bottom of the lake.

The mountains of the national park rise directly to the north of the dam, and the northern shore of the lake falls under the protection of the National Park Service. Therefore, the dam itself and most of the lake do not sit within the bounds of the national park. Yet the Appalachian Trail literally crosses the top of the dam on its way into the Great Smoky Mountains, where some of this world-renowned trail's iconic summits and most breathtaking stretches are found.

StockStudios/istock

Taking to the Waterways

Traveling the waterways of the Great Smoky Mountains is an entirely different way to see the park than most visitors are accustomed to. While the oft-traveled scenic drives and day hikes whisk you up to the highest elevations in the park, the water-borne avenues of the mountains take you to the very bottoms where the gradient levels flatten out just enough for the countless rivulets and mountainside streams to flow into each other to create rivers.

Given the steep grade and wildly varying elevations in these mountains, there are in fact relatively few large rivers here. If you take to the waterways, you'll most likely travel along the Pigeon River. In the upper reaches of the Pigeon River, it is smaller and swifter in character. Whitewater rapids are a common feature, requiring swift maneuvers around obstructions and sharp turns, drops of several feet, and sizable waves. The lower reaches of the river are wider and calmer, more conducive to floating than white-water rafting, providing a tranquil and serene opportunity to appreciate these mountains from an entirely different vantage.

Synchronous Lightning Bugs

Photinus carolinus–as in Carolina–are a very special kind of lightning bug (or firefly, depending on where you are from). It may be that these are North America's most popular insects. People travel from all over the country and the world to witness their light show. The males begin to flash in unison, a synchronized spectacle of bioluminescence that has become an international sensation.

Although it is essentially impossible to predict when peak flashing season for the lightning bugs will occur, it typically lasts about two weeks in late May to mid-June. It is a phenomenon that can be seen in other parts of Southern Appalachia, but the lightning bugs in Elkmont have become the stars.

Kevin Adams Photography

Synchronous Lightning Bugs 87

Islands in the Sky

In truth, the peaks of the Great Smoky Mountains National Park are modest in height when compared to mountains on a world scale. Even among the mountains of North America–the Rockies in the West, or the ranges in Alaska–the Smokies appear relatively stunted. Though they have been whittled down over eons of wind and rain and the upheaval of the ice ages, this makes them no less spectacular to surmount. Standing atop any one of the Smokies ten tallest peaks, it feels as if you are standing on an island in the sky.

According to the National Park Service, the highest peaks in the park are, in order:

1. Clingmans Dome (6,643 feet)
2. Mount Guyot (6,621 feet)
3. Mount LeConte (6,593 feet)
4. Mount Buckley (6,580 feet)
5. Mount Love (6,420 feet)
6. Mount Chapman (6,417 feet)
7. Old Black (6,370 feet)
8. Luftee Knob (6,234 feet)
9. Mount Kephart (6,217 feet)
10. Mount Collins (6,118 feet)

It is perhaps upon these tallest peaks that the true grandeur of the Great Smoky Mountains National Park is most evident. As we stand on top of them, with the forests and the rivers beneath our feet, the wild imagination, the ruggedness that lies deep within the forests of our hearts, and the mountains within our souls, is set free. And it will be with us, all of us, forever.

ABOUT THE AUTHOR

Andrew Kyle Saucier is a freelance writer and photographer specializing in travel and the outdoors in the American Southeast. He lives in Chapel Hill, Tennessee.

ABOUT THE PHOTOGRAPHER

Tony Sweet is an award-winning photographer who offers photography workshops across the country, including in GSMNP, which he has photographed extensively. He is the author of five how-to books published by Stackpole. He lives in Eldersburg, Maryland.